Arc & Sill

Arc & Sill

Poems
1979–2009

David Lloyd

Shearsman Books
& New Writers' Press

First published in the United Kingdom in 2012 by
Shearsman Books
50 Westons Hill Drive
Emersons Green
Bristol
BS16 7DF

and in the Republic of Ireland by
New Writers' Press
61 Clarence Mangan Road
South Circular Road
Dublin 8

Shearsman Books Ltd Registered Office
30–31 St. James Place, Mangotsfield, Bristol BS16 9JB
(this address not for correspondence)

http://www.shearsman.com/

ISBN 978-1-84861-211-2

Copyright © David Lloyd, 2012.

The right of David Lloyd to be identified as the author of this work has been asserted by him in accordance with the Copyrights, Designs and Patents Act of 1988.
All rights reserved.

Contents

Vega / 7

Arc & Sill / 27

Change of State / 67

Taropatch / 93

Coupures / 111

Notes / 149

Vega

Lo sai: debbio riperderti e non posso.
Eugenio Montale, *Motets*.

Lyre

Your late star tracks back
    to its appointed place
all the dissevered points of light
    breath notes slipped from phase

A bone lyre in the dark
    stringless still
        in the dark
heart framed, bone horned

Wishbone struck with promise
    bird toned in the morning hours
at your touch I strum
    breasting the dark

a trilling wire in the breath
slices what remains

Vega

ashen seed
    laid out
        on the lintel

whatever door passed through you
nothing
        flowed outward

unmourned
    motherclot
        clenched in the gorge

no tear
    breaks in you

one tooth only
    struck from your mouth

unyielding

a brass jug
        in the entry
branded
        the brown hydrangeas

brittle petals on the edge
        of parting

utterance
        stopped in its neck

this bone tattoo
        rattles the dice
on the drumskin

all the enumerated outcomes
        star scores
                gauged on the membrane

    this is your world out of water:
        a mud slick at the lip
            indifferent
    mouth crammed with seed

    fruitless fodder
        in a noisome place
    full of rains
        and naming

    as a lid stone
        lifts
    and settles

    I live on
        penumbra
    of your wounded bone

first incision
       of the soft issue

soft stuff
       under my hand
takes shape
       from me

tissue of mis-
       voiced prints
you who do
       not fit slashed

cast off
       threads sticky with seam
rubbed
       wrongwards

    the crystal fluting
        flights
            of wounds

amber-ichor
    aligned
on the workbench

            dredged
              clear

the fingernail
    ringtests
for the voice drill

the shrillest cry
    stalled
at the rockface

cinder paths
        of singing school
gloomy with broom green

print pressed
        in black ash
negative die
        moulding the raindish

and suddenly as light
        broke through

it was as if the wind
        moved as light scattering
motion along the path

and then the bright shower
white shadow fading in the light

day's residues
        ferried
from the banks
        the salted ropes bite

and torque
        a knot-raft
flotsamming over

a door slammed
        in the night
shadows adrift
        hazing
the fanlight

a tissue curtain
        blown across

on the bee-stair
      by the web shreds
dry amber curl
      signal drilled

knotted
      in forgetting
this cascade
      from the latest call

almond drift
      on the air

stress lattice,
      dance net,
dying out
      on the way down

Irishish. Grey.
      The sudden swan-
         duo, creaking
incises the slate

hinging
      this door you are
others
      step through it
stories in hand

word-burdened
      weirdened
with telling

of numbers,
      brandings

from the pain archive
        in the dimmed room
                mole-eyed
in the halflight
        (in the klieg light, blinking

the silence
        incomplete
broken by the sobs
        and cries of prisoners

tapping
        the fissures
in the passive weight

what sleeping rocks
        dream of: space and stone

I opened my mouth
      and was unone:
so many mouths
      leaving their lips in me!

date-scored gash
      the pursed scar sung
into the seaming

What speaks through wounds
      sifted the white stones
and I was undone
      with responding

noneplussed
      and tongueless
in a body full of holes

I drew a thin thread
        through pain, deep
in the hide
        the gathering mole-

work blindly, a sharp
        inhalation of breath
through the teeth
        so

backstitch, back-
        stitch in the spine
slashed with his own strings

hooded,
        through-sounded, lip
split into singing

lolla tongue
        lalla tongue
vacant mouth
        crammed with song

Is this a voice
        you call
a person or a thing?

an almond stone
        unstrung
                let loose
off the eddy

the voice adrift
        graining the slick
with its drag

your same star fades
        at the shoulder
cypress and pine
        fret the skyline

this translucent shade
        fading in brightness
rainweal
        pressed in the ashpath

You who were constellation,
        clearing, beat
play this in dismembrance of me

in pieces
        for my unforgetting

the bone fork rings through

Arc & Sill

Ear

The ear has
        the contours
          of a ruin

a rim opening
        to hurt

the heard
        shock

breaks

a ringmesh
        over the slick

The absence resonates
        with what went down

Two Quartets

      I.i

    quick

scattered
    these tiny beads
across the floor

how to gather them
    into the liquid bulb

where measure
    stems

I.ii

it is not
      true

the plumb lies
      unused

to this plane

      swings
          & is still

I.iii

holding to hurt

      and thrown out of yourself

as a net
      cast blindly
against the spray

I.iv

they come on
        one by one
cresting

to fix one
        like a cite
and it breaks

                shingles

II.i

The story is shy
    trailing
        across the skyface

failing through the lightgates
    its gravitas
sleeps through my fingers

utter
    precipitate

breath sore
    in the gullet

II.ii

The free zone (space
    contracts:
       a room
          a niche
       a coign
of vantage

music from the back room
    (she plays on

fingers wedged in the crevice
    breeze tuned

II.iii

Out of words
back there
yawn yourself
into the cloudscape

dark with night rips
the wind tears in
nothing

the clearing
the cleaving

II.iv

relief
    (as in bas relief
       an exhalation
thrown into relief
   against the skyline

(the lightness of ash
   lifting in the hearth

that tower with the shattered step
   abrupt
      brink
stone
     ateeter

Fade

The tears in things
        Smoke threads the tissue

the fading linen frayed
        to the shoulders

(the truth of him, his
        faith to the object

ash slips from the ring

the persistence of the dream
        in the jacket's frayed shoulders

lingers a smile, a smoke-net
        fraying from the lips

smoke marbles the air

hand to the brow a precise
        space for the other

loyalty to things
        in their vanishing

            i.m. Michael Rogin, 1937–2001

Eclipse

for Nuha Khoury

eclipse
      of a stone
beached
      sand dressed

it draws light
      curtaining
disfaced arc
      that it is

and looks back
      in the eye

drilled
      blank

Sill

A Hand

I

A hand,
      gone

(I loom forward
      to the flank

the watermark-
      welted sheet

(sand cast
      the shredded hour

stroked the spine keys
      to the cleft

II

Tautened membrane
    at the hairline

shift it will
    shift it must

the light sifts
    appalling

what remains
    the labour

(the act split
    from the work

unhooking
    the clasp

(the scalp
    torqued

III

brittle bloody silk
        over the shear wound:

a gap in my wall
        where the stone fell away

falling
        still falling

and calling
        a ghost to the gap

ghost
        of a pleasure

the pleasure of
        a ghost

at my table

IV

the bruise plaque
    spreads

by dint of boot
      again, again
on the same stain

downcut
    the pad

the stone-eddy
    corrades

lay your scooped head
      to the indented sill

grit in the ear
      the bit
           bit down

Tinos

I

The terraced isle
    is marble
to your mouth
    a greeny sill
breaks the north wind

the salt weave mats your hair
    a grief twined
        in a grief

White doves slant across the wind
    on a too bright sky
        no clouds, too few
    dry clouds over
a burden of steps
    the baked shelves
        stone after stone

too old
    to bear

II

A weird wind in your teeth,
    your salt-caked hair

in the wind's cuff
    shuttle and dodge
a scratch staggers
    across your lens

(salt and oil
    drew your mouth

what do you see
    you saw
    what do you hear
the needle jams in the flaw

to steal erotic joy
    from the day

III

wet
      the twisted towel
braided
      at your gullet

the voice box
      squeezed
         to drip

oil and salt
      chafe the throat

This is the full penelope
      she steals
         erotic joy from the day

death splintered
      into constellations
the time line shattered

IV

the isle is full
    of voices
        (what do you hear
at night when

the north wind
    strums the cloud base

in the clear light of noon
    which is not

lath thin
    the tympanum
      athwart the sill
    strums

and you are sand
    against the white sheet

sleeping

V

a stone troop rolls north
        along the gulley
the hardened tears
        mark the lintel

o my savaged children
        my ravaged hide

a dust fume
        lifts from the rosiers
the still damp flags

salt tracks
        tauten her cheek bones

a wind dried eye
        withholds the downpour

VI

The doves were blown about the sky
        lost bitter blue of the sky
some intense mosaic rule
        in disarray
to the puzzlement of angels, maybe,
        this fury of disappearance

step up the
        unstridable steps
a northwind
        streaming in the cloudbase
marbles the blue

the cleated cables strum

something too old
        the noon-scorched layers
an ill wind bears down

the shutter slams
        in your face

Sill

I

A hard sill divides the land:
        the waters spill off
in all directions

Now you are throne velvet
        and wisteria veil
in the endless assizes of parting

All the misplaced abandoned things
        frame the unfit bedraggled ones,
array of the fallen away

This white scar you withhold
        is the inner frame of your skin:
waters break at its ridge, falling

(as if an angel, cavorting
        in exultant flight, faltered
and pitched, baffled by piercing

the unimaginable inner wound,
        a feather's hard curve falling
out of the sheerest sky

II

Eyestone, you are that see-through
    you step up out of the brightness
light-flawed film against the screen

light writing, you calque me
    into a language I am loving to learn,
into the words you teach me to love in

syntagm of steps across the flags
    o grammar turned in the changing flesh
your graffiti's promise carved in my door

III

Dawn trails a ravelled sleeve across the sea:
      the drizzled street
tightens the sky like a canvas.

Weary with stretching
      the heart thins to a tympanum,
a wild song strums from its tautness

startled, scattering, the flock spreads
      and veers, reverse constellation
starring the sky with wingdark

stone archipelago, provisional,
      throw without name, your heart
is a stone set among them

IV

through your gesture the air grows viscous
as if a wing stirring the air into being
carving the curve where there was none
this curve of your lack by my side

your eye thickens the light
as if sight were seeing itself seeing
a feather falling across the sky
deepening blue against the blue

intolerable silence where you were
drums in the ear, tympanum
stretched to attention, reaching
for the steps that beat through the din

V

Mouthstar, your uneven rays flare and protest
    yet the wound was foreseen, as if
it was always prepared to meet you
    stepping up into its fierce enclosure

willingly you greet its sparse gift
    of focus: all the filmy
unravelled threads of your unrest,

the fraying, unsettled fragments
    of the discomposed, gather
and assemble in its rough eye.

Unexpected constellation, aperture
    where the dark finds its darkness,
the sewn lips their suture,
    ragged seam of the star-white scar

VI

strange, how an absence breaks us open:
        is it the sheer scalpel of parting
nicking my taut skin, stored resin

bursting, congealing, a gem
        fraying the light into threadsongs,
fretted lace of our speech?

kernel that thought itself a shell
        breaking open in its turn
a white song spinning off

into the dark of what's to come:
        out of a backdraft buffeted
by passing blades a bird

spun in the sun, white leaf
        on azure, turning, falling
fascinating skypearl, all

your power is in your wound, the grain
chafes in your keeping

VII

Things fall from the sky
this bright feather, say,
from who knows what
remote disaster

over such desolate lands
you step, sole trader,
swayed with bearing, salt
cargoes in your eyes and that

inexplicable smile
no landing shelters

VIII

A stone wind
sheds its whorls:
entail of feeling
torn into place

your salt print
scores the sheet
seams and rips
the straightened cloth

Change of State

for you,
 who are not the origin,
  but the destination

Carbon:

time
and again
you rejoin

there was a life

and you resist
bear

The wind makes for empty spaces in your ear

The airload shifts its weight across the pressure bars:

We're that uneasy on the surface of the earth,
Falling back on human claims

A step in your heart, it comes with you and
Bends with the wind.
I do want it and head for the post.

So far it comes with you and you name it friend,
The span bursting in relief
                        at some distance

The onion tears. Pare back
address
to the encore.

From a charged air
you split.

Out it must
the door ajar

It is the hard lust to outlast

The live drill etches a line from the plate
It burrs like a morning bell

You render the image, yourself still
wrapped, gave me the lift

Taking off from you across the room
half drawn to look back

It is the daylight folding up at the edges.
The bulb wastes itself before dark.

Cast

The delight, as you step out, for the thought
of coming back to the work soon, bathes in
the delay before the white will come to
between the traces. It hovers about
the middle sea, reluctant to strike out.
The jib flaps, with the beating of panicked
wings that you hold out unsteadily. Held
so long at the same pitch the notes
weaken: catch again the faint chock
of the stone knocked from the wall,
the spiral fall of the feather filling out
the gap with slowness. The stone as was
falls, further, is in the knot of the mesh,
the block in the heart of him. At this sill
he wavers, would waive the sureness
of the red path, in doubt of the net.
To be sure, the approach could be sideways,
with charm warding maybe and the
fear net keeping the fear at bay,
that the coulter skate the surface
laid bare by it. Yet sideways
against the keel the breeze
till forces the prow forward.
Out of the criss-cross chop the stem
throws up a spray that frays out
across the wake, blurring the lens or
staggered back into that open v.
         Suppose
below the sand drift builds up
on the humming cables, a weight
sifting in where the voice first faltered.

In that bar the stem of the waves' eccentric
pulse, meshed in reticulate patterns,
and I incline to single down, cleaving
to interference on the far side. For now
some scales are struck off in the cords,
in each cast a single history rings out,
star light and moving in itself. The same stone
is struck again, and a clear break opens
where the shared hand is cast.

Medium

That is your own voice, insisting
on the playback. The figure
of the woman crosses between you
and the picture, shifting the still life.
But it's as if she approaches at night,
unfamiliar and holding your heart in hand,
that's how it starts, only as a car
coughs off again from a stall. The firm curve
of the flyover tears back into the mist,
filling the gap where there wasn't any.
At first it's an outline and then
you're on it, the projection almost
the track retained. And if the rear screen
stars now with a light flawed rain, it's an image
of violence we hold up, patient and
evasive, like when we told the old lady,
"we can as easily fall and break our necks."
The suspension is deathly, reading the cards
on the long distance journey, long as you like.

                There you find the gap
in your life, death or the not having known it,
and hang fire on whether it's what you
feel you need or what you want, the
oblivious object of invidia picked off,
and yourself rounded. Quite little and
shaken, he made for his father's lap, who
fondled his shock, sustained by the radio
going into the afterlife with a strange voice.
If the cards suspend you, those voices are
always and a little ahead with their

restraining murmur. Like honey from out
the strong they get all over till she
does you earth damage or in a real mist
in Reuland, coughing from a seasoned throat,
you weigh up the composed indifference
of the ode against the speechless Roman death.
The poet is all what doesn't survive
selection, it pauses at the knots,
rubbing back up against the forward grain
of history, where evening your own
loose end leaves the world a technical break.
The odds rush in there in a starry fray
like sparks enamoured of the gap thrust through,
and the flesh grows patient. So the quiet
and unexpected intimation of your death
steps between you and the familiar screen
as the voice you refused to admit
played back, or the words that were
for others only, engaged, say, mortal.
You take her up so, and with her
you take death on into your fort.

snow from the east

danger and saving
under one blanket

one love

out of many

Change of State

I

Only begin, as if from O, although in troth
It is the scholar lisping Aleth tracking back
The mumming Pseud across the border to the shapes
Of things. Disturbance stirs among the shadow bands:
The nowhere man's peeling off the light like transfers
While the Pseud laps away around the figures.

It is the Pseud that fascinates, his dazzling sheen
An inconstant lure to Aleth. So he delays,
Hovering above the keys, or thumbing the logbook,
For every appearance of the Pseud, who will,
Perhaps, ease up his passage to forgetfulness
Through the play of many lights upon each other.

We may not come back to them: twin blades they revolve
Turn by turn as caustic figures over the gate
Setting each other forth in over-againstness.
But the unrest between them, that takes you down now
To the fitful stirring that urges to the break
Surging over and over through the swarm of noise.

II

From a confused noise they stretch out their hands, singing
Is believing and they believe a steady state
Lodges in these transfers. Rumours of contentment
Jam the cells, sweetness in the throat fades quietly
To such a delicate refrain, you will come back
And back, as if a finger tapping at the wires.

This is the politics of dancing: go out for
Returns, the circuits settling into a warm song
Calling up resemblance from the lines of the hills.
The perfect tourist sniffs the air, it all comes back
To this for that, and turn by turn, wipe the honey
From your opening lips, others' words give you away.

Once more the sun of artifice arises, on
A warm sill they hesitate in a keen disquiet,
Untold figures spell out a momentary break:
Through this you descend, likeness fraying from the rim.
The delay is formal and insists over and
Over, attention condensing in a brief space.

III

Go forth and divide: what an absurd song, it stinks
In the ear, dwindles and swells as the track narrows
Behind us, lifting away from a gathering spoor.
Slumber is riddled with understanding, something
Like rhythm rises from the breaks as what happens
Passes in between us and never does take place.

From the breach in the strong, such honey. How it gluts
With promise, spewed out into the cells for future
Restauration. Smeared in the wound, sealing it heals,
They say, smothering the gash with limpid amber.
Their voices extol the limpid, separating
What it is you want as if the dance but rendered.

Your voice tacks the broken steps, is small through the din,
Declining southward on a rumour of amber.
And would fall out into clear crystals, but that it
Changes again as a tinctured finger warmed up
The purple dust into a violet mist, filming
The glass with silver in an abrupt change of state.

IV

In a grey dawn awakening and maybe this is
The famous pass. Pitching high we are sung through yet
In a minor key and play it over and again. Dub dawn
And the mountains slope downwards cut off by the frames
The tumbling light brims over snagged in the brakes:
It's the old story deep recollection sneaks in

A streaky slick with the glimmer of boiled out ink
Trails back and we call it anxious hunger. The break
Is here if ever, too true we all want to be
Rounded, but if you don't attend that break takes on
A morphic voice, like to the lark at break of day
Aching for the new moon and to be of the cusp.

On the rim of their voice you step up, hungering
For what slips between the doubles. Utopic dreams
Dissolve you, to the figures taking untold paths
Where you are powerless and would delay daylight
Under the fraying rains. Step back, her eye gives back
The distance where it detaches and fans away.

V

And as it pares off it's with the reserved sound
Of the fabric shearing, a remote must-spoor
On the brink of the foregone. Take it from the draught
In passing, it is as if they slip into place
Where the misleaders thrashed out some kind of clearing:
The unheard-of tries for the rear of the sunlight

Set on the way from off a faulted track. All changed—
By mere citation—we hesitate on the step
Of what we were. Is it in their words? to bring us
To this pass, and southwards, the shimmer of delay
Withdrawing. That which will not meet us saps our strength,
Slipping unguarded into the enemy's habits.

Listen, it is the bulk of the world cascading
Over the selvedge in a confusion of light
And plunge. Though to rearwards is held out, the way is
Between, where the figures wedded in shadowbands
Lift apart in a moment of parting in which
The ground unsettles underneath the detachment.

VI

Hey, poet, say, what is it you're at? I make space
As in Matera, in the midday sun, dwellings
Step back from a white noise. Space rends like a split pod,
Shaking out the precious spoor on the arena,
Not a random squeak troubles the arrival, time
And again a like flock motions some constellation.

Hey, poet, what are you getting at? Honey spreads
Like the swarm sips from his parting lips, a rumour
Leaks through the components as an odorous snatch:
Riddle re me, riddle re me, she comes too late,
She speaks awry, and what she asks is where you've been,
And what you speak is where she ends and turns again.

She speaks ajar, the aggregate asunder: render
The cacomeme babble towards the fourth star,
Form resists and saps you along a further limb,
Music drifts out on the draught, notes let loose tumble
From the keys and through the frame. From off the level
The piano planes over an azure expanse.

VII

All the museums were closed and so we missed the tomb,
Drawn away now to aesthetic power. The grass grows
Greener where there's something missed. Honeydew ice is
Cool and cheap and life the better for it, rinsing
Backtastes from uneasy spittle. How they reserved
The figure for himself alone, suspended

In a dry dark, as the voices of the walkers
Fade to a confused noise, pausing, hesitating
On the path. So an unmappable gap folds under
In the unbroken plane, while loose ends unravel
Through a sudden draught. Out of this space the flicker
Comes to light, look how his soar's like likening,

As a clear song rose ahead of the swarm, urged on
By the spirit of the hive they diminish to
A fleck in the blue—alive, alight,
                                    arrested:
If he gives one more random peep, give him a sharp
Knee bend right in his transfer characteristic:
To a white noise he's broken, and a door clicks to

VIII

Out of the tiniest break, a wave say, it rises
To the one who listens, ear atilt and at risk
To the gift of opening. Where it parts, the blade twists
And will not cease, turning
                      Trennen ist dichten, he says
And we see him diminish along the platform,
The sundering tracks singing slowly together.

We decline in the series, stepping in the print
Of the others, as one on a dark stair and downwards
Out of the brittle light. Step back from the swell and
From the things which have no ending, in the breathing
Of spray we are small but through us it fans away
Over the firm surge. It's as if I hear the rain

Drenching the dark green, but to that there's no return.
The friends are gone over and in the space they left
We step, the suspension of the ferry widening
Across the channel. For the moment it is ours,
The passage: they have left us our voices, singing
A concentration of the ear against the wire.

    *

Tipped towards a rinsed sky
A mouth full of drills
And he can't place my voice

Soft rain against the pane
But it's not the same

The white bird slides in under
The cloud, dividing the waters

He is rooting around my tongue
And then the rubber she stretches

No, they came to me, neither
Are they mine either

Accent grave
Acute

And then there was that moment, the one
in the overshaded garden, as we sat
on the grass, in the sunshine, the air
still rinsed with recent rain and the shrubs
alive with it, talking, taking that air.
                                      Can you recall
the pungency of basil, it rises from the spray,
from the brown bag, and here I am
thinking to make you dishes of white pasta
reeking of this green herb. But you're gone now
and can't be at my table.
                      Sometimes it seems
too many have gone, and always
at the wrong time, or in the wrong way
till we begin to wish their fate on others,
less close but nearer at hand.

Even the whole of what we want
is simple, the evening light green
through the vines, reading,
the comfort of your mother's creaking chair:
the pleasures transfer, are common,
escape us.
           Too many are gone now,
to the south, to the east, beyond
the horizon of lamplight.
                    So many
they no longer count, as ash still drifting
after the technical storm; too many
to be buried apart.

And as I came to you,
in the morning, to touch you,
it was your body I missed, the whiteness of the linen
was too much in the stripped room.

Taropatch

you are defined
    in parting
        as a wave

In a too harsh glare
You were bleached out of
Any shade & reached where
Light shadows

The margins through bleed-
Ing slivers
Of sharp reed
Blades my fingers

Now run along
To the tune of hurt
If the notes are wrong
Then rightly I flirt

With your after image
Among other shades al-
Ready you edge
Away beyond recal

The reins jerk from a long desired command
Arms flung out against the silvery glare
An over-eager angel hurtling forward trips
On overplus of darling speed, hasty sinews
Melt in the glare of sun-dazzle, thank-
Fully his footing stumbles at peak of vault &
In terrific consternation that urgent point
Of bright is dashed into breakers & douses
Through the criss-cross play of sea light.
Salt bites at the smooth nude's wounds: I
Grow even to fear the gathering of their
Womanly hands tending to his multiple lesions
Unclenching his ragged grasp & his attention
Bled off in a tattered curve towards death
Sieved away with a see-saw song while above
The fixed sphere sails off into unconcern

What a vain cloud he plucks hold of, look it
Floats down the river in the morning mist as
A cover for his errant imagings, lithe &
Pink he goes on calling it, as blood thins
Out in the stream. That's another diversion
From the jumpy heart of the matter, only
The vein of what he really wants leads back
To that hub bub, where there'd be nothing
To say, only hum sometimes perhaps I'm here
To stay: not at all, he babbles on, wound
& wound on the same track, his attention
Spun out to a light & fine tension that
Snaps & he leaps to fuck with what seems
To answer his desire. & thrashing through
Folds & folds of candy-coloured nebula
The last twist is, she doesn't back off
Just stands still there where she always

Ah given to drink mandragora, & a broad
Yawn gulps at the empty space that's
The gut full of hankering rubbing up
Very close to mortal fear for a stopgap
Gone for good now & in a reddening
Dawn gobbling up the darkness I want
You now & the long running sore flares
Shedding its lurid gleam beyond the edge
Of visibility one little while & then
No more, it flares up & is gone. From
The initial flush it is bled out to the
Farthest margins, the abrupt of apartness
Soothed with a balmy haze blurring off
The hairline between the name & who
Falls under it seaming a shifty fault, lips
Pouting for contact at the end of the line.

Once upon a wasn't he all full of himself, quite
Indifferently glancing through the grove, but
Shrieks he in recognition & it's an ear splitting
One, the sound carries, nor will this trail of
Spittle part from lips lapped in a bitty parting
As the likeness peels away & stays just the same,
So doesn't that moving stair stream down from
Where I last caught you half-turned in suspense
Before the gangway. But to struggle back up what
Runs out from you, like she flowed in his face
Coming back with his own words, it does hurt
To tear away & not lag back to grasp maybe
Just an echo in the passages saying it does blur
Through the tear always, home burns & it is hard
To dare a way from this hot haze on the horizon,
The tear crusts to salt traces forged in afterglow

The stain glows ochre & the wall
Steps outwards where your shift
Was hung up for the last while, I'm
Poured through that gap, a yellow
Smear on the edge of twilight & won't
Condense, thinned out through the
Watery pale to keep the distances
Covered at every point, what was
Apparently & could yet be coming up
Over the dissolving limits, there
I'm suspended & will finger the stops
Of breath, the reeds bend into slits
Leaning away from attention as they
Mark out where the lurking exits
Drop away from your sight on the far side
& I fill in your figure passing there

He melts from the seat of his power
Into the nervous gold shower: her
Threshold is sunlit, his bronze tower's
A pod split to scatter him tingling
& the desert bursts into a flowering
Beyond anything he can reach out to
O how her suddy & delicate limbs
Shimmer & fuzz his valued standards
To slaughter in the noonday haze, &
Reduced to subterfuge he sneaks
Orders along the folds of the land:
The shining block is beat out thin
To take up the scattered points, the
Wafer glows along the skyline light
Leaf flaps in the breeze & I can't
Lay hold on its flickery gold transfer

The pine boards drip with a sexy resin,
That humming is the dimmer & bodies
Looming up through the lowered light
Fade off into various well oiled limbs,
The switch dips & my eyes swim through
Fashionable movements, the fishy flanks
Dive from my grasp, resinous strings
Swelling in the pit & slop on out
The open window as anyone's delight.
The amber light is thrown all over
Working bodies longing to come on
Every nerve you even see them touch
At the highlights: you're caught up
In amber to my tacky eye, held &
Again the warm light melts off, now on
The table bathes our tendered hands

Surely this small green should be enough as
An island in the torrid stream, the shoots
Spill from the table into loose strands &
The stem grinds to rest in the bay. In
A green shade, skim duckweed from the pool
Brimming over through the moss mat. The iris
Fringes those dilatory depths, hardly a breath
Troubles their reflections, mouthing the fruit
As it plumps & the saps bed in under the tongue,
There's poetry in that there gob they murmur
Hugging a snug narcosis, easy dreams of home
And honey lap their limbs in a heady trans-
Piration like limed with light through emerald.
The jaundice spreads in his satiate eye, turning
At the heart of all those faces the true gem twists
In a further island, nursing the invidious hanker.

Myself delighted but desiring more a stay, you
Hang on in the salty thicket, bounce the bag
In your free hand & shear bubbling delight
In the black fruits from off the tangled branch.
To tear away is long drawn on, harking back
For the final look, you white say against the
Darkening mass, snapped up at the very last
& mounted against the blank. But the road
Simply will not bend, mindless the while you're
Declining to a smaller body, my glance refused
Till the prince of rays leaps out at length
From the unseen, you're gone into undergrowth as
I'm verging on another outlook, hear your
Laugh skim back in with 'only look to the sea
For motion', the race streams off below, streaked
With phosphor & flecked with a starry foam

The lure is to come on straight when
Honesty is a sargasso mat that dips
Would turn turtle as the swell bears
Down & you're washed instead with my
Warm drift as I'm overboard hugging
Two contours to me as one while a
Drizzling headland breaks up in surge
The low one backs up out of shingle
Where the nations slide under in the
Backwash. I see ahead & rearwards
Through a broad arc the furthest waves
Must fade somewhere around my heart
As a frantic singing in the azure
Sounds so clear on a taut wire
& the flock rises sheer from the gulf
In something very close to panic.

In grey wool & at your hem almost
Brushing the dusty hedge in sway
Of passage now a phenomenal fog
Muffles the long drag of casting off
From any clear shoreline, plucking
A few strings to the shuddery throb
In motion as slack waves over
The channel blur off into suspect
Horizons, a faint burr on the zinc
To work from in the middle of things
To begin with no fixed marks drawing
The predicted curves out. Hood the cape
With silence, only such intervals
Buzz with static, set directions in
Suspense, & peering down to bone grey
A tremolo modulates out of reach.

Now it's back to writing letters demanding
Should I let all spill out directly as if
Run on towards the margins like it may
Fall out or tune every phrase to a nice
Effect, a choice discrimination held in
Reserve: see, my I's are oblique strokes
& signs of worry pricking at the page
They're stacked up against what's also
There to be picked out but they slip in
The way I see things, the distance grows
Comic as you'll be gathering strands I
Would never even take up as loose ends
Knotting & unknotted in your curious
Threading back into what lies behind
These near-random designs that I'm now
In the very middle of composing.

Whittling at the dark root
In anxious hunger he
Hunches astride the stream
& gnaws his nether lip,

The parings litter its
Violet sheen cast off in
A detailed measure of
Surface flow & eddy.

Only the swallow swerves &
Crosses your sense of a
Controlled lapse & bending low
To touch level, even

The ripple slips from
The tickled lip. We watch
Your white smile undefine
Greying against the pitch.

The gut strums & plucked as a sticky thread
Through the laps draws in the wanting lips
In passage to close at last with the missed
Face. But his bruised heel aches, it's too late
To not look back from the shoulder & check
Strung up with doubt at the brink of a light
Suffusion, the seam closes up in a rocky face,
Surface glitter folds a pretty useless figure.
You recall his left arm drawn across the brow
As if the black stream swells over the view
Or he's washed from place with all the other
Details that tracked out into the possible
Swim as radiant markers now gathered up in
One vague body swirling across the line
Of current, he feels for those strands only
Where they tend into the viscous channel

Coupures

Coupure

Daylight sifts in effortless silk over the outstretched palm

Dividers size up the pane: frame for me
The impossible leap across the Coupure

Birth of low mist swirls from the channel, light as if light
Teased strands from the liquid, or gusts of dry sand along the beach
& inland gulls sip the surface of buildings smeared into burred glass

Your dancers shift still through bands of shade: the lines
Translate across the page like so many fluent tongues
& the grids superimpose, the stark cranes beyond the fence

Strung out now between transports, et passager,
Friends dot the map all over, cut figures of desire

Shuttle between the friendly hands, & unpick the threads of the
     passage after

Oostende 3/12/78

Song

so still through lips
he would not name
her he loves thinking such
a thing profane

out through lips would
song but rise sounds
in motion could then break
silence now her bounds

Under the Influence

The cloudy wafer is coloured with ripple effect,
creamy ice as we see it lifting across the channel, like it flows in under the facial muscles &
the lips rise to sip the sky

     The desire is to write like
     Cross-currents marble the surface
     Darker blue above the weed
     The light streaks measure
     Speed of flow & ripple
     Like the blotchy skin
     In contact all over &
     Mottled with the currents
     If you step back
     Focus is tricky & slips

as from the irises along an opted gradient—the
objects are all gleams on this slice of life listing off like a wedge on the cobbled market &
roll like smooth pebbles along the bed. A clear
stain spreads through the litmus, the matting is
alert with forethought, tuned as ever to the seep
of the salts through the pores & imperceptibly
shifts. The tapes are all loopy & snag your vulnerable heel: trust is indeed implicit but turned inward which is steeper as you step off onto
the shining floor. Limewash came off on the fingers, a tracing in the prints from the retiring
room; equally the sanding brings the nerve ends
to the surface & blurs the impression in the powder. They flick through the files & find 'frustration'. The photos sneer & are gone like mug-shots under the smeary thumb. The urge to detect

implies them already in the system. But then so
too does the figment of blur as they rush through
the frames, as if the not quite there really did
slip away from the focus, back through the nets
like watery prawns. Those wavery palps turn in on
the meal, all red & amber & gelatinous. Their
outer limit is said to be sensation, pain the
limit of their suffering. They blush though on
the hot-plate, & the filaments run back into our
codes of conduct, making the network buzz with a
savoury indignation. Our highpoints glow in the
cirri thinned with wind & come on like cuts in
the fabric. Look how the firmament streams with
colours as you leap for the shreds & the threads
float off on the horizon in a watery sky, nobody
's delight.

The expanded day extends a calliper over how much
oxygen the brain needs, while it drains off thin-
ly as pulses at either end. Drawing a low profile
along the contours of a doze, anxiety slithers in
in terms of babbled examinations & the erotic gla-
nce accusingly reversed. That he ruffled your hair
was a tender gesture, crinkling the features into
a contented smile, but try to grasp his body as
the series of figures. They split off at the bla-
des in two wings, doors line the corridors & the
agents sortie with multiple devices to sneak into
the future, acting out the hidden intents of the
ensemble. The music wafts in from the green room
traversed by circulating conspirators & the couple
remains suspended in the vestibule. That conjun-
ction runs back under the skin, ultimately every
desire feeds back to the same switch which is nuc-
lear dread, the charming gnashers stained with
stimulant acids. Fear coats the nostrils like a
universal coke smear, threading the atmosphere
with leads & they snort at the traces. The snot
is a sullen armature. The alarm strikes in his
pith & bucks at the sudden touch, the sick float
bobbing through the surface tension as a gob in
his throat. I don't care if I'm fucked, but I
want you to have to see it. Look, the photograph-
er feels no fear, his function is above that, his
flash plugged into all the other pulsing wires, &
anyway the little brats jerk below his anaesthet-
ic boots. The facial mask would be personal hyg-
iene at the pouty lips, the blade can go on in re-

mote from panic stations. Considerate hurt plumbs in a new gash & screws it hard against the four walls as the red wounds group on the horizon & gabble of dawn raids on the bleary white eyes. A tribal dance thins the brainstream & it filters back into itching muscle. Why not write with the toes & leave the fingers room to think? Intense groupings blotch the passage over the map, nomads shadow the steppes & the blackened fields catch on with travelling flares, scorching runnels traversing the rootmat. The outer smoulder steams off in smoke trails like a fading spray from the meeting waves of hunger. The noodles sifted through the soup infused with flavours. The local hot points are peppers & fire the tongue to seek relief in liquids, washing the buds with palatable saps. The exoskeleton peels off, the vulnerable pulp was 'purely me' out of the filtered tides.

No place for Truth capitalized, even the living columns hover on the pale & sexual light of the 'clear day' they stand out in. The multiple is merely a masking tape, & they stretch into the distant times orderly as divisions ranking past & future. Molten gold was threaded into the foundations & seams gleamed in the mortar. Mother mother they cried & drained away the vital flux into the soil. I guess you remind me of my mother somehow, & I imagine the father isn't so far off either. Larded with jeux de mots the points are dinned into him on every flank. They grace the sheets with an amber light that spills on out the window, taken out there for some guy's good fortune glowing in the wind. This ache diffused through every nerve glides in under the slip of the person as I know you to be, & streams in loose braids over your figure as feathery touch grazing the slope of your ribs. Curved bodies loom out of the landscape wafted in on orogenous vocab. The tattered hems of the new state are borne out on that breeze, the selvedge fraying off in threads into the grainy air, a historical pregnancy from any point of view. Turn up osmotic desire & the channel fuzzes with seepage between components. On a glad day the alloyed rain falls through me, & the screen is flecked with interference. The sky loses its grip on the stars & aluminium, they prick its smooth skin & it blushes at the places of loss & returns. This desire is very close to dread in kindness & the drift of fears beneath the drumming hide is veined with loving blue

The sadness was a vague libidinous cloud condens-
ing at random on the panes. The little droplets
lose their bearings & waver like suckers at the
threshhold. Then straggly plasm licks the dust
& crusts off into a black scab. Pushed out at the
edge of the rush to arms as so much for biology.
The third person enters masked with erotic threat,
you know you dread the grinders, mashing on through
these broken-down jaws. A filmy image it passes
across the scene coated in black, moreover it
flicks the crust from the walls in passing so the
ooze bleeds through flesh-hued plaster, meant to
be sightly. But the bare patches are the ghost
of his passage, the corridors elsewhere pale into
momentary insignificance. Out at last, yes, I do
reach after his image, he has my idea in hand &
I dance on according to his invented steps

A.N.D.

The helix burns in every aural cell

You give a name to my desires
And energize my bounds

Ear to ear, in the dark, the music
Passes through the walls, the walls are thin
Here, conducting this translation

So I can leap I guess, and that
Makes up our bond, withdrawn only to con
Template the fineness of your print's
Inverse transfer, turned at the selvedge

Wind sounds cavernous in the branches taking away
Osmotic desire, it all transpires
In the ear, or I can do nothing without you
Taking this down, the other half
Not only in your hands, you are it, reproduced

History as a solution of the self, the image
And the inscription beneath coming apart
Vibrant in the intervals of the pillars his name
Grown abstract, an idea adrift among
The eddying forms and becomes one

Tips on the sill straining through the frame
Beyond his to possess, the vegetal rain reverberates
And the farmdog's barking, at the back of my head
The familiar arrangement slipping out of touch

Looking back on us the fire gathering round us
The system takes over behind we seem to cohere,
The ideal room stepped out from our shoulderblades

As angels of sorts bend at the frame
To draw the types back out of the fluid base

Moved to incline to you by choice of chance

They see us if they do now as figures on the ground

The eyes shade into the lids and feel the warmth
Of invisible waves bathe over the skin

Her ears pricked to sounds away beyond my range
Her coat dissolves into autumn bracken,
At home with signals from inaudible spheres

Subject only through the eddy
Of converse words troubled
By our differences, where there are walls
There there are words getting across the disturbance

The perimeter grid is smoke
In the sun, the light beams spectral
And blends, he diffuses along the lines
Leaning out across the edges with screwed eyes,
These could be a spear stroking the heart of the city

With impeccable care in the lunch hour
This immigrant worker outlined the grid over
Her dead son's picture, so are blocked out
Through every dimension, and the cone splays
Magnified into a giant screen

Chalk dust blurs the curve of the hills,
They slip into unobtainable light shifts, here there's
None of the borders of blood, we're electric
And fade at the edges out of polar discharge

The changeless seeming angels of every cell
And the unbroken passage of the elohim
Folded around every single state transmit us

How we stand in the light of what is possible
And the wave breaks into coloured paths

The gate porters only reserve the overview

History presses round the desk as light fades
Out from the filament, far from it, the field
Is emerald, he spills the knurled gems
Through his fingers, the crystal spirals
Burn in unattainable halls of silent light

O if I could I'd surely spend my life in the light
Of all your presences, it glowed through every cell
And the bounds all trembled, laughing, ridiculous
In the happy confusion of sonicated membranes

Why so many joys, even shared ones, escape us, skipping
Into imperfect sunrise, ragged wings breaking into the column
Of reflection stripped in over the perpetual swell

Scattered I know and broken, but still I would repossess
All between my hands, temples between the palms, some mirage

But your metamorphoses must be endless, delight only rises freely
                                                    through them

Goodbye then my scenario is studded with your forms

Your presence lingers like scent from off a
Land full of angels I can't get out of my head

Parting I drew the mask down over my head, face diffused
Along the meshes, one strand took my place among them till I fell
Down through sleep into a dream of condensation

Outside light skips between the leaves, I've had to leave so
Measureless fields waver dotted with thresholds,
The road limits shift the smoky glass contains
And drift across loss to chance on your various contents

All inspired with words, your names I repeat endlessly hover
Strong and delicate pinions in a clean sweep over
Airy spaces, the empty fields petrified to emerald paths
Of stillness, strung out in a taut canvas
Of nerve ends, all my gates flung wide open

Pebble heart of flint with dry fingers I could stroke
Sparks into the chalky air, it sped from the sling
To lodge as a third eye, spinning quietly to the path
He will survey the murmuring fields with stony gaze, feeling
He feels no more, but breaking down, grit in his teeth

The ridge is pain in the warm half-light, low-
Flying swallows say, the depression's on the way back.
The figures of desire dim in the dew haze
Flicker along the tracks and go out at the gates

Back to things like Venus and / the sole star in the sky
It's the haze that does it, the alcohol coursing the veins, we're
Knotted up in all kinds of transport carrying us away

This fever is retarded, they've already slipped under
The burning wings, the scorch mark comes part of your make up

As things fall out, the blade twists over the calling gateway

The same hunger signals all of us closer

The blocks move with us slowly up the spiral. The uneven edges
Ache for completion. Eternity is endless space.

The confusion of tongues trickles at the base,
Power weighs as a wedge in the fracture, the grains
Accumulate, we're all mixed up in words and powerless

'They're all we have though, your gestures are so
Ambiguous' as if you come to me as if you are
Rinsed in light rain from friendly contacts as if I respected
A vision of the infinite city building through your openness

As little discs they stack up in every vein, the burden
Is ancient, the crystals receding into the seam, their
Spiral core goes back so far, while the body's immediate
The present scars us knowing the discs span so much
Time, and the first word makes up a painful departure

Sister to the stars the night is closing Venus
Slips from the moon Lost between the constellations
Invisible face among the dissolving shades, the figures
Smeared into the half-light. Looking after the cherished footsteps
The last touch drifts out of reach The corridors glisten with pallid eyes

Under the hatch he fingers the veins The rockface oozes
As occasional tails of light The light hem trickles across the granite
His intact skin splits across the step, & how the unexpected angel
Span the gates out wide into the city night

Like your laughter echoed along the shaft The tremor fluid
And the tense oil spread across the plate These domestic arts
The tacit stripped across the raw. Flutings waver at the curtained frame

Bring out your gentle flame into the dim, the hearty warriors
Are deserting, their boots bruise the sand. It fades in the definite glare

Against the foreshore the regular swell your blessed shores

The pain is abstract, for nothing you could put your finger to

The bridges are down all along the passes,
Embattled villages retreat into mountainous silence

The hurt splits in the seed, what flows down under the skin is
Like waves phased over the sanddrift, like the landslip,
Like oil poured out across the smoked pane

The drops follow the same paths in the slipstream.
Thanks as you help me to step in through the next screen.
But your face grows dim from the ledge out:
Vanish under the skin as another reflection

The rescue teams grow bored and resentful, snow
Crumbles under their feet like sand, or the ultimate corpse
Is not reward enough. Come on then, throw yourself
Across the crevice, the spine spreads like wings in the ultramarine,
The cantons laid open to the raids of the angels

I finger the binding Coming together we churn up the deposits
The spirals relate the fragile bonds, debris littering my palm
Like febrile wings in the interstices like shed scales like lead
Dropped from the fractured tower, it draws into cold spheres in
                                                          the moat
Your voice at least will sing along the wires until the city

Attention bent over the glossed margin I reach for the edge and
                                                      you're not there
The terra incognita webbed with guesses Surrounding likenesses
Pace out his distance from her You were gone at the bridge
He looked back and she slipped from view at the shoulder

Langorous fins stroke the saline Sink through the clear
I grip the sill In passing air the sheets crust with salt
Hanging on for you and the groaning hemp torques at anchor

Eyes that drift through the mirror The northern seas
Break on the absent headland I gestate webs like sheets of spray

Angel of labour you lead on like pillars of cloud, of fire

In the absence of borders, the ideal flower names flourished across the
walls

Foam laps from the bucketing hulls Veins of liquid
Marble I look for nothing beneath as it blends its million globes

The canvas dark under the blazing walls. They kick his teeth
For his quiet smile. Rooftops like blades against the curved dunes
Infused with shadows they haunt him as the loss of his own

Indigo cut with black through the small frame, stone dissolved in ink
He floats out on distance, strange traffic enters like unknown speech
You rise in him like spray settling across the spur, on the horizon
Shimmering crests & they sing out the joyful islands

Wings litter the sky, nowhere to go & baffled with freedom
Purchase had seized the father's house as ever, wares
Laid on the trestles. He scatters the notes & the doors
Gape like sagging pillars, the staggered lintel, like anger searing
The body of silence. The roof folds & they belong like smoke into the
city haze

His the only breath he cannot hear. As if I was her dissolved into the thin air like smoke. It hangs over the ash, over the cup, over all that remains of the night & the plants drink in all that lasts of it. Their cells revolve like dials through undivided times.

& the angels have folded their wings like scarlet flowers foreboding rain. Set them on plateaux & on trim lawns where the slow change slips like glaciers onto the plains. The hidden intrusions carve into the flesh.

They stretch across the falls & with their bare arms they fail once more. Feet slip on the algous boulders; which side is the truer is the only question they suppose.

Desire accelerates. They dash down the cobbles,
The stage revolves its struts crumble as three points of his logos.

Alone, immersed, he draws it out to stain the sheet

Light sears even the blind skin, darkness is ample, we can
pretend to fade. The sheets are grey with persistence.

The quest had disappeared already into the thicket, a braid
of hounds sniffing the air. To wake like that in the morn-
ing is all they ask. The sad tales do not lap like that.

Remember the gulls swooped through the azure. The boat
bobbed like no more than a buoy in that expanse. Yet they
seemed so small, so perilous against the skyline, the swell
nosing up out of the depths. So alien you had to call it human.

All he feels are fabrications. The sepulchre draped with
a thousand cloths. He opts gaily for the switchback, but
suddenly it is bottomless, & fear grips him as a mirror.
Dawn, twilight, they are only the shifts of light across
the ground. He took note of every change till no state
seems probable. They dissolve from underfoot like loose screes.

A myth she sleeps on the far side of the hedging. They had tried for years to get through, & when at last he finds the only stream, how should he start to bring her out?

Work Lines

There are always two men at work
At least in the writing
& elsewhere
They seem to touch each other easily

To come & part
As parts of the machine
They work with
Glow with a mauve fire

The foreman is an old crow
With his gulp & nervous touch
He handles my body daily
Eight hours a day

Loose limbs thread through the tired eyes
Hallucinating beauties
In the pretty bands of stress
With all the colours in the arc

Spanning a tiny sector
Finger & thumb
& there is no more point
In the work than that

The bits glance
Sparks off highlights
In the grey face
With the flash of contact

In Suspension

"On dira: 'c'est son style,' mais croyez-vous vraiment?"
Denis Roche, *Dépôts de savoir et de technique.*

r voice like glass on the point of breakage, she hangs alread
goes off to play pinball and I sit with his coffee cupped & m
smell of urine and sand descending from the Caserne, throw me
like the deliberate ignorance of his encounters with place &c
strangeness evaporates where it was expected, visibility in f
rhythm of my desire so hectic & of hers so taut & slow that w
lust as much to be desired as of my own desire. And in fury
two histories cross in a knot of fears neither of us are real
like glass on the point of breakage, she hangs already on the
two hours waiting on what should have been an excellent spot
dex, duckrabbitduckrabbit—the order is quite arbitrary, the
so when he came in I asked if he really was the friend they h
lackbird singing in the blackthorn tree' this evening by the
resents so many blocks, & I find all sorts of little ritual a
seem to change so much more rapidly—clouds scudding across
my slight disappointment. Then on the way home met this guy
Bouhaddiou Hamid/Delannoy Marie Odile 92 rue Jean Jaurès 59
is is a day Of darkening symbols, when nothing is merely its
& caught his sleepy looking eyes, the glance of the good drin
ying on his back, all soaped up, it would lie hard against hi
w far my attraction for other people depends on their attract
ation, past the patient prostitutes — The chips I'm guzzling
So much rubble here, piling gradually out from the sites, the
ong thighs of the model on the moving ad panel for topless sl
plus signifiant, c'est l'absence de l'étape 'zéro' dans " La V
ckground of noise in the cafe and I can't quite make out his
breakage, she hangs already on the quite maternal figure of t
d & my beer. Whoopee! Bleep, bleep, & then all the sirens ar
ther traffic spins by outside, & when he stops playing the ma
descending from the Caserne . . . e most difficult to penetrate
with place &c.   Intersects all too closely with my own condit
d be slobbery kisses, his lispy mouth close to mine, 'you mak
lusory sense of such immense possibilities curtailed by dates
isibility in fog conditions remains at a constant distance. A
low that when they do meet it's perfect, when not, irksome &
ternal figure of the plump Mme G. reciting now "Escape into L

where else. Some other traffic spins by outside, & when he s
row me back against the wall & to strands in Sligo, the Atlan
the quotidien & the practical always the most difficult to pe
too neatly as a whole with my own condition as I fictionalize
istance. And as once anticipations might have thrilled in th
ound and this deer seem plain images of the desire of the man
til they slammed the brakes on, & we rode straight on through
licking through the pages like a card index, duckrabbitduckra
ving, washing, going out for a coffee; and how in almost unbr
or a cigarette, and then asked me to go to the Maikumba, fant
ted and, doubting, knew the infallible sign Had left him unma
uld I make a long stride and you on my back from the peep o'
tumbling down the face of the hill the old part of the town b
dry flits in white stains across the green. His skin smooth
he skinned kidney in warm salted water for a couple of hours.
one already on the late train to Paris, I have his address &
es personnages mêmes, se passe par moyen d'un entrelac sans a
petition of good lines. Her voice like glass on the point of
beat in the Algerian cafe, to the background of strange accen
ry kisses, his lispy mouth close to mine, "you make me feel I
her the buzz of all that unbroken spread of soapy skin, a vas
he roads with an old lecher from the county of Mayo and he a
kin being a forward stimulus to the drowsy palps. Borne off
n them my satisfactions are elsewhere, seasoned with exhaust
sing topless shifts come to rest with a plonk on the frame eve
oi, uniquement toi, au lieu de te joindre, elle te divise ou
round of noise in the cafe & I can't make out his foreign wor
scribe it from memory — a young man following a girl who has
art's inconsistencies seem salutary & valid, thought the final
20 year itinerary a more precise mapping of the irresolutions
ce de nouveau involve a certain betrayal of all previous conc
is perfect, when not, irksome, & for me an explosion of block
f those rare pleasant encounters that go somewhere else as i
a time I have seen the book, and your name would be in it. <u>La</u>
he first round & he'll pass before you get it all down. Just
scudding across a seascape seen from above is not quite it ye

Blind man you couldn't touch me at all; but as I was saying—
o histories cross in fears neither of us are really expressin
y, the notebook is witheld, & all you see is the glance of th
w writing presents so many blocks, & I find all sorts of litt
imply the fragmentary which traps the erotic urge, the hanker
in almost unbroken solitude one's moods seem to chance so muc
on my way home met this guy from Senegal, who asked for a cig
citing now 'Escape into Love.' The foreigner, her husband, I
ue Jean Jaurès 59 Lille tel 520129. /8.00 mardi /No 4 — dire
How far my attraction to other people depends upon their attr
warn them my satisfactions are elsewhere, seasoned with exhau
lie hard against his stomach, smooth & cool above the suddy p
less slips come to rest with a plonk on the frame every 2 min
éro' dans 'La Vision' de W.B. Yeats. Comme si l'échange de ce
u make me feel like a woman' but he didn't grasp. Thought per
in thing is, it remains a hanker, the fantasy & the desire ar
s kiss' — but the intention weighs down so heavily on the vac
time I have seen the book, and your name would be in it. <u>Lame</u>
he sirens are really in the machine. No where else. Some ot
pletely at a loss what to ask for: the quotidien & practical
counters with place &c. It intersects all too neatly as a wh
he friend they had told me about. No, but as we settled in t
Perhaps in the morning, lying on his back, all soaped up, it
delusory sense of immense possibilities curtailed by dates /s
conditions remain at a constant distance. And as once antici
she creeps through the grass Alone, important and wise And li
en they meet it is perfect, when not, irksome, & for me an ex
sire should be realized in the fantasy, or the fantasy become
inker, with whom perhaps to spill out over the edge of all th
ce of the waitress coming with the first round, & he'll pass
ritual acts to palliate them — shaving, washing, going out fo
boîte de nuit. I didn't — would I have if I hadn't been writ
throwing eyes to the right of you and eyes to the left of you
one hand, the wish to penetrate & get to the finish, on the o
haps to spill out over the edge of all this repetition of goo
he know that his pupils Will pass from change to change, And

thrown open the shutters of the window behind my desk, & catc
finger curiously among the fine red hairs, they catch gleams
0 minutes to wait for the next train. The tiredness is a sli
well rolling in great clumps of seaweed to dry off along the
aving the novel as a series of gestures towards the profound,
cise mapping of the irresolution of moral experiments than th
n explosion of blockage, lust as much to be desired as of my
of all desires that are as these. I have read them in this w
stories cross in fears neither of us are really expressing, &
as if they picked up from some other time before. So we arra
ass out before you get it all down. Just flicking through th
so many blocks, & I find so many little ritual acts to pallia
is morning with a fitful fantasy stirring though my doze, of
hose sleepy eyes have grown fatherly, distant, I remind him o
creamed "J'en ai marre" from beside the door, & I was eager f
like as we climbed the streets of the old town after & browbe
d be the deception complete. On the one hand, the wish to pe
alps. Borne off beyond the scope of my attention now, only h
much rubble piling slowly away from the sites, the grass can'
ence de l'étape 'zéro' dans 'La Vision' de W.B. Yeats. Comme
tu aimes et tu n'aimes pas, elle fait de toi ce qu'elle veut,
he a woman-hater from the day of his birth! And what do they
kiss' — but the intention weighs so heavy on the vacant symbo
back over the kidneys; serve with croutons of fried bread. E
spins by outside, & when he stops playing the machine, the wa
found, constantly intimated, never really engaged. I'm still
falsification — the speed of the novel's 20 year itinerary a
delusory sense of immense possibilities curtailed by dates, e
If he was different, what would they find to talk about, will
range to meet, & that's the beginning of something else. Bou
n't hear much of the station traffic any more, & even with th
littering like so many prisms on his white skin. Then leap i
cognition immediate in the close air of the seminar room, & a
they had told me about. No, but as we settled into the round
their attraction for me met its limits in the force of his de
one hand, the wish to penetrate & get to the finish, on the o

lecher does be telling over all the sins he committed, or may
when he stops playing the machine, the waitress starts the ju
ll these labels confuse me when I'm out shopping — completely
prove the procedure or not: can be the intensification is ano
rained your gentleness To acrimonious care and, to be strong,
so nervous, but you know that's really sensual, the way she t
ich is for the woman', and 'the desire of the woman which is
coming with the first round, & he'll pass out before you get
Maikumba, fantastique boîte de nuit: would I have if I hadn't
t night, a light breeze through the slats cools the dim room.
leap in my hand, his spread legs tensing & relaxing as the gr
mouthed the mucous oyster from the end of his proffered fork,
buzz of the voice tickling the ear, & it's a shock to see her
soak them in salted water for a couple of hours. Cut the ski
lose to mine, "you make me feel like a woman", but he didn't g
lit up & break back in little bits glancing across the smooth
ever ends, just because it must be broken to be touched at al
only his address runs off my pad now in a low key hanker to k
can't grow. Envision a city growing so madly towards its ide
es mêmes, se passe par moyen d'un entrelac sans aucune suture
ce que tu veux, elle te prend, elle te laisse, elle te désire
there's many a thing you don't know about the heart of a man.
the waitress starts the jukebox. This blue aquarium light, t
nal effect of the novel's a series of stopping to take notes
e has allowed to pass Without one gesture to the loneliest on
vaporates where it was expected, visibility in fog conditions
: would I have if I hadn't had to write today? Don't know. S
stirring through my doze, of his soapy body stepping from the
s ideal form that that ideal can never be realized, for all t
he grey drops mingled with the soap. Roll over, it dries on
one hand on the glass, the other touching the child, the vein
ng, denied Love's only eloquent proof, the irrational caress.
didn't grasp, thought perhaps I meant that's what I thought I
et to the finish, on the other the buzz of all that unbroken
low key hanker to know what still could be going to come out
of the train home, the splinters of any brute encounter lodge

Notes

Collected in this volume are several previously published chapbooks:

Taropatch (Oakland, CA: Jimmy's House of Knowledge, 1985)
Coupures (Dublin: hardPressed Poetry, 1987)
Change of State (Berkeley, CA: Cusp Books, 1993)
Sill (Los Angeles, CA: Cusp Books, 2006)

All of the above chapbooks can be viewed at Eclipse, courtesy of Craig Dworkin: http://english.utah.edu/eclipse/

Vega (Los Angeles: MindMade Books, 2009)

Individual poems in this volume have been published in *Conjunctions*, *Angel Exhaust*, *Poetry Ireland Review*, *Beyond Baroque*, *Masthead*, *FreeVerse*, *Skald*, and *Past Simple*.

Poems from *Change of State* were set as songs by Hao Huang. A recording can be found at Wild Honey Press, courtesy of Randolph Healy: http://www.wildhoneypress.com/

The sequence *Change of State* draws freely from Maurice Maeterlinck, *The Life of the Bee*, and from Rene Thom, *Mathematical Models of Morphogenesis*.

Vega is the brightest star in the constellation Lyra. The sequence *Vega* draws freely from an essay by Freud on Jensen's *Gradiva* and on the *Oxford History of Prisons*.

www.ingramcontent.com/pod-product-compliance
Lightning Source LLC
Chambersburg PA
CBHW031150160426
43193CB00008B/312